Combating Child Abuse

Guidelines for Cooperation between Law Enforcement and Child Protective Agencies

Douglas J. Besharov
Rapporteur

The AEI Press

Publisher for the American Enterprise Institute
WASHINGTON, D. C.

1990

Distributed by arrangement with

University Press of America
4720 Boston Way
Lanham, Md. 20706

3 Henrietta Street
London WC2E 8LU England

1 3 5 7 9 10 8 6 4 2

AEI Special Analysis 90-2

The AEI Press
Publisher for the American Enterprise Institute
1150 17th Street, N.W., Washington, D.C. 20036

Printed in the United States of America

Contents

Foreword

Across the nation there is a growing recognition that law enforcement agencies must play a crucial role in protecting abused and neglected children. Almost every state has passed a law requiring child protective agencies to notify law enforcement officials (either the police or local prosecutors) of certain more serious types of cases, usually involving significant physical injuries or sexual abuse.

At the same time there is much uncertainty about the best way for law enforcement agencies to use their extensive legal powers and operational capabilities to help protect endangered children. This report seeks to guide state and local policy makers by describing how law enforcement agencies—in cooperation with child protective services—can channel their efforts within communitywide efforts at child protection.

In addition this report is meant to be used in training and technical assistance efforts designed to upgrade law enforcement and child protective services for the victims of child abuse and neglect. As such, it serves as a companion volume to the American Bar Association-Police Foundation pamphlet, "Child Abuse: A Police Guide."

This report was developed through a consensus-building process. It involved a nationwide group of law enforcement and child protective experts similar to the one used to prepare *Child Abuse and Neglect Reporting and Investigation: Policy Guidelines for Decision Making*. The centerpiece of the process was a set of two policy conferences of leading law enforcement and child protective administrators, policy reform advocates, experts on various substantive issues, and key government policy makers. At the first meeting a preliminary draft of this report, prepared by Douglas J. Besharov, was reviewed by the entire group. Based on that review, a second draft was prepared and a second meeting held. Subsequently a revised draft was sent to all participants for their review and approval. Revisions were made and circulated. Throughout the process unanimous decision making was required. The final report was the culmination of this consensus-building process.

An advisory committee of cooperating organizations aided in the planning and implementation of the project: Robert Horowitz and Susan Wells of the American Bar Association, Susan Martin of the Police Foundation, and Betsey Rosenbaum of the American Public Welfare Association. The government officials who helped plan and organize the project were Jane Burnley, director of the Office for Victims of Crime, and Betty Stewart, associate commissioner of the Administration on Children, Youth and Families. Harvetta Asamoah and Elizabeth Fish provided the legal research on state laws for this report.

DOUGLAS J. BESHAROV

Participants

Ira Barbell
Executive Assistant
Office of Children, Family, and Adult Services
South Carolina Department of Social Services

Thomas Birch
Legislative Counsel
National Child Abuse Coalition

Jean Bower
Director
Counsel for Child Abuse and Neglect
D.C. Superior Court

Larry Brown
Director
American Humane Association

James Cameron
Executive Director
New York State Federation on Child Abuse and Neglect

David Chadwick
Director
Center for Child Protection
Children's Hospital
San Diego, California

Robert E. Cramer, Jr.
District Attorney
Madison County, Alabama

John Duffy
Sheriff
San Diego, California

Michael Durfee
Medical Coordinator
Child Abuse Prevention Program
Los Angeles County Department of Health Services

Jeanne Giovannoni
Professor
School of Social Work
University of California, Los Angeles

Margaret Gran
Cofounder, VOCAL

Norma Harris
Program Associate
National Child Welfare Leadership Center
University of North Carolina

Jane Jagen
Police Child Abuse Investigator-Instructor
Friendswood, Texas

Beverly Jones
Senior Field Consultant
Child Welfare League of America

Ellen King
Detective
Sex Crimes Unit, Detective Bureau
New York City Police Department

David Lloyd
General Counsel
National Center for Missing and Exploited Children

James Marquart
Assistant to the Deputy Commissioner
Services to Families and Children
Texas Department of Human Services

Joyce Mohamoud
Executive Director
Parents Anonymous

J. Tom Morgan
Assistant District Attorney
Dekalb County, Georgia

Janet Motz
Child Protection Program Administrator
Division of Child Welfare Services
Colorado Department of Social Services

Howard Pohl
Assistant State Attorney
Sexual Battery/Child Abuse Unit
Office of the State Attorney
Miami, Florida

Lieutenant Tom Rodgers
Indianapolis Police Department

Rebecca Roe
Assistant District Attorney
King County, Washington

James Skinner
Chief
Police Division
Omaha, Nebraska

Carla Strouse
Director
Children, Youth, and Families Professional Development
Centers
Florida Department of Health and Rehabilitative Services

Sergeant Toby Tyler
Crimes against Children Detail
San Bernardino County, California

Michael Weber
Director
Hennepin County Community Services Department
Minneapolis, Minnesota

Hubert Williams
President
Police Foundation

Charles Wilson
Director
Child Welfare Services
Tennessee Department of Human Services

Federal Officials

Carolyn Becker
Project Monitor
Office of Justice Programs
Office for Victims of Crime
U.S. Department of Justice

Jane Burnley
Director
Office for Victims of Crime
U.S. Department of Justice

Carol Petrie
Social Science Program Specialist
National Institute of Justice
U.S. Department of Justice

Betty Stewart
Associate Commissioner
Children's Bureau
Administration on Children, Youth and Families
U.S. Department of Health and Human Services

Susan Weber
Deputy Associate Commissioner for the National Center on Child Abuse and Neglect and the Office of Discretionary Grant Programs
Children's Bureau
U.S. Department of Health and Human Services

Organizers

Douglas J. Besharov
Resident Scholar
American Enterprise Institute

Robert Horowitz
Associate Director
Center on Children and the Law
American Bar Association

Susan Martin
Project Director
Police Foundation

Betsey Rosenbaum
Project Director
American Public Welfare Association

Susan Wells
Research Director
Center on Children and the Law
American Bar Association

Acknowledgments

This report results from a consensus-building conference conducted by the American Enterprise Institute in cooperation with the American Bar Association, the American Public Welfare Association, and the Police Foundation, under a grant from the Office for Victims of Crime, Office of Justice Programs, U.S. Department of Justice. Additional financial assistance was provided by the National Center on Child Abuse and Neglect, Administration on Children, Youth and Families, U.S. Department of Health and Human Services.

This project was supported under Grant No. 88-VF-GX-0004 awarded by the Office for Victims of Crime, Office of Justice Programs, U.S. Department of Justice. The assistant attorney general, Office of Justice Programs, coordinates the activities of the following program offices and bureaus: the Bureau of Justice Statistics, the National Institute of Justice, the Bureau of Justice Assistance, the Office of Juvenile Justice and Delinquency Prevention, and the Office for Victims of Crime.

Additional financial assistance was provided by the National Center on Child Abuse and Neglect, Administration on Children, Youth and Families, U.S. Department of Health and Human Services.

Points of view or opinions expressed in this document do not necessarily represent the official position or policies of the Department of Justice, the Department of Health and Human Services, or the other cooperating organizations.

1

Joint Child Protective Responsibilities

Child abuse and child neglect are community problems requiring a cooperative response by law enforcement, child protective, and other local agencies. These agencies share the same basic goal: the protection of endangered children.

Child protective agencies seek to protect children through the provision of services or the removal of children from the home. Law enforcement seeks to protect children through the arrest of offenders and criminal prosecution. These approaches are complementary, not incompatible. Depending on the situation, either agency may benefit from the assistance of the other. Accordingly, many child protective agencies and law enforcement agencies across the nation have developed working arrangements to call upon the other for help in meeting their responsibilities toward children.

This report places primary focus on law enforcement and child protective agencies because they are primary agencies that receive and respond to reports of child abuse and neglect. To be effective, however, both types of agency must be aware of and work with various community services such as women's shelters, child abuse prevention and treatment programs, substance abuse programs, and various public and community health programs.

Progress and Problems

Since the early 1960s, all states have passed laws that require, under threat of criminal and civil penalties, a wide array of

1

professionals to report suspected child abuse and neglect.[1] These mandatory reporting laws and associated public awareness campaigns have been strikingly effective. In 1963 about 150,000 children came to the attention of public authorities because of suspected abuse or neglect.[2] By 1972 an estimated 610,000 children were reported annually.[3] And in 1986 about 2.1 million children were reported.[4]

This twenty-five-year expansion of child protective efforts has saved many thousands of children from death and serious injury. The best estimate is that since 1975 nationwide child abuse deaths known to the system are down from about 3,000 a year to about 1,100 a year.[5]

But there are still major problems. Depending on the community, 35 to 50 percent of all fatalities attributed to suspected child abuse and neglect involve children already known to law enforcement and child protective agencies.[6] Many thousands of other children receive serious injuries short of death. In New York state, for example, the reincidence rate is about 25 percent.[7]

An important next step in building child protective capacities is to ensure that the full, complementary capacities of law enforcement and child protective agencies are channeled to maximize the protection of abused and neglected children. In some communities the need to develop cooperative structures has taken on added urgency as the problem of drug addiction spreads to tens of thousands of families.[8]

Child Protective Agencies

When reporting laws were first enacted in the 1960s, they were based on a model child abuse reporting law promulgated by the U.S. Children's Bureau.[9] The model law recommends that reports be made to the police, largely because in every community they are available to receive and investigate reports. Most states passed laws to this effect.

Soon after the passage of these early mandatory reporting laws, however, states began to expand the social service agencies that were already providing child protective services.

These child protective agencies have become the primary recipients of reports of *intrafamilial* child abuse and neglect; all states have amended their reporting laws to require or allow reports to be made to them. The vast majority of reports are made to, and are investigated by, child protective agencies.

Child protective agencies operate in the social work tradition of helping people with their problems through a variety of mental health and supportive services designed to assist parents to care for their children adequately. Based on their investigation of the home situation, child protective agencies assess the risk to the child, evaluate the capacity of the parents to care properly for the child, determine if emergency services are required, decide what social services are needed, and then offer such services or arrange for some other agency to provide them.

A small proportion of all substantiated cases (including those that go to court) results in the child's placement in foster care.[10] In the rest there is a continuing assessment of the care the child is receiving while the family is provided a variety of needed family-based services. Although always in short supply, such other services include financial assistance, day care, crisis nurseries, and homemaker care, which are used to support parents and to relieve the pressures on them. Parent education services, including infant stimulation programs and parent aides, are used to give parents specific guidance, role models, and support for child rearing. And individual, group, and family counseling and mental health services are used to ease personal problems and the tensions of marital strife.

Moreover, to the fullest extent possible, child protective agencies seek to obtain the parents' voluntary acceptance of services.[11] Only if the parents do not accept such treatment services, or if it appears that such services will not adequately protect the child, are services imposed through court action.[12] A small proportion of these cases results in a civil or juvenile court action, and an even smaller portion results in criminal court action.[13]

3

The Need for Law Enforcement Involvement

The criminal justice system plays an equally important role in a communitywide program for the protection of children through finding and reporting cases, assisting child protective agencies, investigating cases, placing children in protective custody, arresting perpetrators, and prosecuting offenders.

The symbolic importance of affirming the norm against child abuse requires the criminal prosecution of some cases; criminal penalties serve as a community statement that such behavior toward children is not countenanced.[14] Law enforcement can provide the necessary authority to assist the child protective agency perform its therapeutic role. And in certain circumstances arrest and criminal penalties can protect children more effectively than social services because they can better deter further maltreatment.

Furthermore foster care is sometimes improperly used when the child could be adequately protected by jailing the offender. Many children, for example, are placed because the mother's live-in boyfriend is dangerous, and she seems unable to prevent him from returning to the home. Thus the removal of the suspected perpetrator from the home may be an important child protective option. (Parents, however, should not be prosecuted simply because appropriate treatment services are not available in a particular community.)

These realities have led to a growing recognition that arrest and prosecution of offenders are needed to protect some maltreated children. The most widely known of many recommendations for the expanded use of arrest and prosecution in child abuse cases was made in 1984 by the Attorney General's Task Force on Family Violence, which recommended that "family violence should be recognized and responded to as a criminal activity."[15]

Complementary Responses

To draw a dichotomy between treatment and punishment as the respective approaches of child protective and law enforcement agencies is therefore somewhat artificial. The criminal justice system can provide important rehabilitative services as well as punishment to reinforce the wrongfulness of the parental conduct. And a civil, child protective proceeding, which can involve the child's forced removal from the parents' custody and the involuntary treatment of parents, has indisputably punitive aspects. Moreover, whether or not there is a criminal prosecution, a child protective agency investigation is needed to determine the needs of the children.

Society does not respond to all crimes in the same way. Different approaches are developed depending on which agencies are better suited for handling a problem. In protecting maltreated children neither law enforcement nor child protective agencies have all the tools that are needed.

An effective response to child maltreatment requires cooperative and coordinated action between child protective and law enforcement agencies. As the Attorney General's Task Force on Family Violence pointed out, "no agency or program can be successful working in isolation. Each must recognize the interrelationship among the legal, health, social service and educational responses to family violence."[16]

Often the involvement is interactive. Jack G. Collins, former commander, Juvenile Division, Los Angeles Police Department, points out that police action obligates agencies concerned with rehabilitative programs to become involved.

> When the police take juvenile victims into protective custody and/or arrest adults suspected of inflicting traumatic injuries on children, the attention of other agencies is automatically focused on the problem. Prosecuting attorneys, criminal and juvenile courts, probation departments, and other concerned social agencies must necessarily perform their assigned duties. This results in an official review and consideration of child-beating cases by community agencies charged with the responsibility of developing and implementing rehabilitative programs.[17]

2

Reporting

Laws that require the reporting of suspected child maltreatment must also designate an agency to receive the reports. In many states the law creates a patchwork of complex and often confusing procedures that make full reporting less likely. Reporting responsibilities should be clarified and streamlined.

Reporting to Child Protective Agencies

No jurisdiction requires that all reports made under its reporting law be made to a law enforcement agency. In about twenty states the law gives the potential reporter the choice between reporting to the police and the child protective agency,[18] but few reports are made to the police.[19] In about thirty states the law actually requires that all reports made under the reporting law be made to a child protective agency.[20]

Moreover, although practices vary, even when the police receive a report, they are more likely to investigate cases of sexual abuse or serious physical abuse than minor physical abuse and neglect (which are handled primarily by child protective agencies).[21] Law enforcement plays no role in most cases of neglect and emotional maltreatment, which together constitute about 66 percent of all cases.[22]

Thus in all but a few states actual reporting practices establish child protective agencies as the principal response to cases of familial child maltreatment. Now that law enforcement agencies are playing an increased role in child abuse cases, this basic service structure should not become fragmented. When more than one agency is responsible for encouraging, receiving, and investigating reports, it is too easy for no agency to be responsible.

Child protective agencies should encourage better reporting through public and professional education campaigns. In addition there should be careful efforts to improve coordination between child protective and law enforcement agencies so that there is less chance of children falling between the cracks as each agency thinks the other is investigating a particular case. And subject to the exceptions and procedures discussed in the next section, all cases of familial child maltreatment should be reported to them, preferably on twenty-four-hour hotlines dedicated for this purpose.

Reporting to Police

Some cases require an immediate law enforcement response, and for this purpose the public should be able to make reports directly to law enforcement. When a child has been murdered, for example, the need for a criminal investigation is apparent. Even in less serious cases an immediate police presence may be needed to stop a parent from abusing a child, to take a child into protective custody, or to prevent a parent from fleeing, perhaps with the child.

While all child protective agencies are encouraged to respond to reports twenty-four hours a day, seven days a week, many, expecially those in rural areas, cannot. Some after-hours reports do not involve immediate danger to the child, and an investigation can wait until regular office hours. Others, though, represent situations of great danger, and the child must be afforded emergency protection. The police must be available to respond.

A few states require a report to the police if the child protective agency cannot be notified of an apparent emergency situation.[23] Iowa's law, for example, requires a report to "the department of human services. . . . If the person making the report has reason to believe that immediate protection for the child is advisable, that person shall also make an oral report to an appropriate law enforcement agency."[24]

Whether or not there is such a statute, this appears to be the actual practice in most places. But formalizing the procedure would help ensure that the police are available when needed. The District of Columbia requires the police to investigate any case that involves a neglected child (which under D.C. law includes abused children) in immediate danger.[25]

Therefore, to ensure that children needing immediate protection receive it, direct reporting by the public to the appropriate law enforcement agencies should be allowed or perhaps even mandated. State law or the local CPS-law enforcement protocol should provide for reports to be made to law enforcement agencies in designated situations (see table 1). These arrangements should be a planned response to a particularized, local need: provision should be made for reporting procedures, for determination of whether an emergency investigation is necessary, for the nature of the investigation, and for the subsequent notification of the child protective agency.

Such separate reporting should not satisfy the underlying need to report also to a child protective agency. For even when there is a criminal prosecution, the child protective agency is needed to ensure that adequate arrangements are made for the child.

Reporting by Law Enforcement Agencies

Because police officers are in the community and frequently in people's homes, they are in a unique position to identify cases of child abuse or neglect. They often discover cases during routine functions such as responding to domestic violence calls or dealing with juvenile delinquency matters. They also receive formal and informal reports from a variety of community sources.

The police are legally required to report suspected child abuse and neglect in all but two or three states. In most of

TABLE 1
Situations Requiring Law Enforcement Involvement

When someone other than a parent has abused the child

When the case appears serious enough to warrant the consideration of an arrest or criminal prosecution, as established by state law, CPS-law enforcement protocol, or local prosecutor's policy

When the child protective agency cannot be reached (such as at night and on weekends and holidays) and an immediate response is needed

When speed is essential and the proximity of the police to the child gives the police faster access than the child protective agency

When a child seems to be in immediate danger and the child protective worker cannot enter the home or the place where the child is located or the parents otherwise make the child inaccessible

When a child must be placed in protective custody against parental wishes

When it appears that the suspected perpetrator may flee

When police assistance is needed to preserve evidence

When police assistance is needed to protect the person reporting or the child protective worker or to otherwise maintain order (when the parent, for example, becomes belligerent or physically threatening)

SOURCE: Derived from Douglas J. Besharov, *Recognizing Child Abuse* (New York: Free Press, 1990).

these states the law specifically designates law enforcement officers as mandatory reporters. The others require reports from all persons, which includes law enforcement officers. The question is, To what agency should the police report?

In about half the states the law requires law enforcement officers to report and provides that the child protective agency is the sole receiving agency for all cases.[26] In these states the police, like all other reporters, have no choice. They must report directly to the child protective agency.

As described above, about twenty states allow reporting to either the police or a child protective agency.[27] In almost all of these states, law enforcement officers are both mandatory reporters and designated receivers of reports, so the reporting requirement has no operative effect on them unless the statute or departmental policies require that reports be made to designated police units or officials or to the child protective agency.[28]

Even where police officers are not legally required to report to the child protective agency, it appears that they usually do so.[29] This is true whether the report is from someone else's complaint or the officer's own observation (for example, while on a call). No law prevents the police from conducting a parallel investigation, but available data indicate that except in more serious cases they rarely do so.[30]

Nationwide, police make about 14.5 percent of all reports of suspected child maltreatment received by child protective agencies.[31] Other major professional groups and their reporting rates are public schools (about 32 percent); hospitals (about 8 percent); social services, excluding welfare, (about 5.5 percent); and juvenile probation (about 2.5 percent).[32]

There has been substantial improvement in reporting. According to the first national incidence study of child abuse, in 1979–1980, police, coroners, and sheriffs did not report about 58 percent of the children whose condition suggested maltreatment, compared with about 44 percent for hospitals, about 87 percent for schools, and about 69 percent for social service agencies.[33] According to a second incidence study in 1986, police failed to report about 39 percent of all known cases, while the rate of failure to report for hospitals was about 34 percent, for schools about 76 percent, and for social services about 74 percent.[34] Nevertheless these levels of nonreporting are still matters of serious concern.

Although there are many reasons for this incomplete level of reporting, this mixture of ambiguous reporting mandates does not help.[35] Therefore, regardless of any action taken by the law enforcement agency, state law or procedure should require it to report suspected intrafamilial child abuse and neglect to the child protective agency. Such a rule creates clear-cut lines of responsibility and communication for the bulk of cases that should be referred to the child protective agency. Even if a criminal prosecution has been initiated, the immediate and long-term needs of all children in the family must be assessed and, if necessary, suitable substitute arrangements made.

3

Assigning Investigative Responsibility

Although the basic framework of requiring initial reports to child protective agencies remains unchanged, more than forty states have passed laws that require child protective agencies to notify law enforcement officials (often the local prosecutors and coroners or medical examiners) of certain cases.[36] These laws are an important addition to community child protective capabilities because they formalize a procedure for involving law enforcement in child abuse cases. They could be many times more effective, however, if their focus were sharpened.

CPS Notification to Law Enforcement Agencies

In about nineteen states child protective agencies are required to notify the police in designated types of cases, and in about twenty states they are required to notify the local prosecutor. (In about four of these states this is in addition to a required notification to police.)

Only about six states require the child protective agency to inform the police or prosecutor of *all* cases of child abuse and child neglect regardless of their severity.[37] Such notification statutes are too broad and thus counterproductive. They include, for example, all cases of educational neglect and all cases of poverty-related neglect. As a result, they burden law enforcement agencies with hundreds and, in large communities, thousands of reports that have no prosecutorial merit and for which they simply do not have the resources to review. Experience suggests that this kind of undifferentiated notification process overwhelms law enforcement agencies with mountains of paper, creating a risk that serious cases will be missed or not be acted upon promptly. Conversely, requiring notification of cases with greater prosecutorial merit serves to flag them for heightened law enforcement attention, making a prompt response more likely.

A greater specification of the cases that should be referred to law enforcement is also needed to prevent the inadvertent discriminatory application of law to racial minorities and the poor. The effect of racism and poverty on the process of reporting, investigation, and provision of services cannot be ignored.

Just as racism plays a role in many parts of society, it is expressed in the child protective process at both individual and institutional levels. Individual racism is seen in prejudicial beliefs and discriminatory behavior. Institutional racism is seen in the policies of organizations that restrict opportunities or access to assistance. Minority children, and particularly poor minority children, are already overrepresented among reported cases and are underserved by child welfare agencies. Therefore clear guidelines should be established that prevent discrimination against disadvantaged children and their families.

The vast majority of notification laws therefore focus on the more serious cases, although there are wide differences in what must be reported. Depending on the state, statutes require a notification for all reports of abuse (about twelve states),[38] "physical abuse" (apparently only one state),[39] injury or abuse "so serious that criminal prosecution is indicated" (about seven states),[40] sexual abuse (about eight states),[41] "aggravated child abuse or neglect" (apparently only one state),[42] "serious injury" (about four states),[43] and fatal injuries (about thirteen states).[44] (Some states require the child protective agency to notify the coroner or medical examiner in addition to the police in case of a fatality.)[45]

In about four states local prosecutors have been empowered to require the child protective agency to send copies of all or specified reports to them.[46] In a few others the child pro tective agency must notify the coroner (or medical examiner) when a child dies of suspected abuse or neglect.[47]

Unfortunately most of these notification statutes are too narrow. It is a mistake to limit the notification requirement to cases of sexual abuse, for example. Law enforcement agencies have as much to contribute in cases of physical abuse, and certainly the children are in equal need of protection. Statutes that limit notification to actual, serious injuries also exclude cases of great and demonstrable danger to children.

Massachusetts, for example, enacted an extensive listing of serious injuries that child protective agencies must report in writing to the district attorney for the county in which the child resides. A report is required if

> the department has reasonable cause to believe that any of the following conditions has resulted from abuse or neglect: (a) a child has died; (b) a child has been sexually assaulted . . . ; (c) a child has suffered brain damage, loss or substantial impairment of a bodily function or organ, or substantial disfigurement; (d) a child has been sexually exploited . . . ; (e) a child has suffered serious bodily injury as the result of a pattern of repetitive actions by a family member.[48]

But statutes such as this leave unprotected children whose parents have engaged in dangerous behavior that through some chance did not result in these specifically enumerated injuries. To take an extreme but not rare example, they exclude cases in which a parent shoots a gun at a child but misses.

Establishing Guidelines

The diversity of approaches described above is confusing and makes interagency coordination more difficult. As noted, some notification statutes are too broad, while most are too narrow. Better, and more comprehensive, guidelines are needed to ensure that law enforcement is notified of cases appropriate for their review. (While absolute uniformity across states is not necessary, greater similarity in approach would facilitate the sharing of information, the discussion of common problems, and the development of validated operational guidelines.)

Some have suggested that law enforcement be notified of all criminal forms of child abuse and neglect. As Rebecca Roe, a member of the consensus-building group for this report, explains:

> Law enforcement has a role to play in child abuse cases where a violation of the criminal law may have occurred. It is law enforcement's function to investigate and enforce the criminal statutes, regardless of whether the crime occurred against a family member or some other person. Reporting statutes requiring child protective agencies notification to law enforcement should refer to cases where the criminal law may have been violated. All states have criminalized sexual abuse cases where the child has suffered serious physical injury. Many have also criminalized cases of potential serious physical injury (various "endangering" statutes), minor physical injury, and some forms of neglect. Mandated reports from child protective agencies to law enforcement should require reports in all these cases.[49]

Unfortunately the dichotomy of criminal and noncriminal is helpful only in those states that have narrowed the reach of the criminal law to cases suitable for criminal justice involvement. In most states, though, all or almost all forms of reportable child abuse or child neglect are crimes. Catchall statutes commonly make it a crime to endanger the welfare of a child.[50] Other statutes simply criminalize "child abuse and neglect."[51] In addition general criminal statutes against assault, battery, murder, rape, and other felonies or misdemeanors are often broad enough to cover all forms of physical and sexual maltreatment.[52] Thus in most states one cannot simply say that "criminal abuse" or "criminal child neglect" should be investigated by law enforcement because this would mean that all cases of child abuse and neglect should be reported.

Hence, in those states where all or most forms of child maltreatment have been criminalized, additional guidelines are needed. The key elements in such guidelines are (1) the identity of the perpetrator and (2) the severity of danger to the child (not of the actual injury).

The Perpetrator. Cases of nonfamilial child abuse and neglect should not be in the province of child protective agencies. Child protective agencies are designed to aid children threatened by persons in their family or living in their households. They have little capacity to protect children harmed by strangers or living in institutions. As the earlier child abuse consensus-building group explained:

> A recent tendency has been to broaden the definition of those who may be reported for "child abuse and neglect," particularly in cases of sexual abuse, to include all adults, whether or not in the child's home and whether or not responsible for the child's care. Cases of maltreatment by babysitters, adults not in the child's home, and strangers are more appropriately assigned to law enforcement agencies. They should not be investigated by Child Protective Service Agencies unless the parents appear unwilling or unable to protect the child. . . .
>
> Child Protective Service Agencies are family oriented. Therefore, although the abuse and neglect of children in public and private institutions is intolerable, its investigation is beyond the scope of functions best performed by child protective service workers. Child Protective Service Agencies should be assigned investigatory responsibility only over intrafamilial or quasifamilial child maltreatment, broadly defined to include parents, guardians, foster parents, and other persons (such as boyfriends

17

or girlfriends) continuously or regularly in the child's home.

The investigation of child maltreatment in out-of-home care, on the other hand, requires specialized units of professionals (often law enforcement or licensing) with the necessary expertise and authority. Furthermore, such units must be independent of the agency or facility being investigated, so that there is no conflict of interest.[53]

Therefore child protective agencies should not be assigned the primary responsibility for handling cases of institutional child abuse or neglect and nonfamilial maltreatment. These serious problems must still be the subject of mandatory reporting, but the reports should be directed to law enforcement, licensing, or other appropriate agencies.[54] If the child or family needs help or counseling to deal with the maltreatment, such assistance should be provided by victims' services or other mental health agencies. Moreover, if during the investigation it appears that the parents are responsible for the maltreatment (or are unwilling or unable to protect the child), child protection agencies should be notified.

Severity of Danger. The consensus-building participants concur with the approach of the vast majority of states that mandate child protective agencies to notify law enforcement agencies about certain more significant or more serious types of intrafamilial maltreatment. A good starting point is the recommendation of the Attorney General's Task Force that law enforcement agencies "presume that arrest, consistent with state law, is the appropriate response to situations involving *serious injury* to the victim, use or threatened use of a weapon, violation of a protection order, or *other imminent danger* to the victim" (emphasis added).[55]

To implement this concept, a three-tier approach, tailored to local capacities, is recommended. On the first tier all communities should provide for law enforcement notification in all cases of sexual abuse and all cases in which the child has suffered serious or significant physical injury.

In addition law enforcement should be notified of situations in which a child is in danger of being seriously injured. The child need not actually have been seriously injured for a notification to be appropriate. Law enforcement should not have to wait for a child to be seriously injured before intervening. The potential injury or danger to the child is of equal concern.

Local Agreements for Less Severe Cases. The second tier involves the definition of potential danger to children. The types of situations considered of sufficient severity to warrant a notification should depend on the prosecutor's policy about which cases are taken to court and the relative capabilities of the relevant local agencies. Therefore state law should mandate that child protective and law enforcement agencies at the local level develop written agreements, or protocols, concerning the other types of situations that warrant an automatic notification to law enforcement. Rebecca Roe notes:

> As in any area of the law, prosecution may not always occur in cases where the criminal law is violated. Child protective agencies, law enforcement and prosecutors should develop written agreements and protocols on the local level that address prosecution issues and how notification requirements should be carried out.[56]

The following guidelines for referral to law enforcement, which were developed jointly by New York City's child protective agency and the Kings County district attorney, illustrate how a local consultative process can integrate this concern for both past and potential injury:

1. all fatalities
2. all head trauma injuries (that is, subdural hematoma)

19

3. all injuries involving ruptured organs, unexplained abdominal injury, or other injuries consistent with abuse
4. all fractures that are unexplained, multiple, or in various stages of healing or where the reason given for the fracture is inconsistent with the injury
5. all second- or third-degree burns, cigarette burns, or other burns consistent with abuse
6. all lacerations to the face, external genitalia, or extremities that are unexplained or where the reason given is inconsistent with the nature of the incident
7. all lesions on different parts of the body
8. all nonorganic failure to thrive
9. all cases where any physical injury to the child appears to result from abuse
10. all cases where there has been one previous indicated report within eighteen months involving the child named in the current report or any other sibling or child living in the same household
11. all rape, sodomy, and sexual abuse cases or attempts at same

Some observers have suggested that penal codes be narrowed along these lines to delineate better the types of cases that should be assigned to law enforcement. This, however, would restrict the ability of prosecutors to take protective action in special situations not covered by narrower statutes of this type.

Additional Case-by-Case Referrals. No rule or guideline can cover every situation. Many seemingly less severe cases may be appropriate for law enforcement involvement. Hence state law or the local CPS-law enforcement protocol should guarantee that on a case-by-case basis child protective agencies are free to refer any other case they deem appropriate to either police or prosecutors, and they should be encouraged to do so.

As described above, states differ on whether the notification should be made to the police or to the prosecutor. In general, notifications should be made to police agencies because they are better positioned to conduct investigations. Differing local capacities may, however, suggest that the prosecutor be notified.

Prosecutorial Discretion. Prosecutors are responsible for determining appropriate case dispositions within the criminal justice system. Therefore state law should give local prosecutors the authority to obtain copies of any individual report or designated type or types of reports as they are received or at any time thereafter.[57] (Such requests should be in writing.)

Timing

States also differ on whether the notification should be made immediately or after an investigation. In about thirteen states the child protective agency must notify the police only after its investigation reveals specified types of abuse.[58] But waiting to involve the law enforcement agency until an investigative determination is made precludes a truly joint investigation and may make it less likely that evidence is preserved for a possible criminal prosecution. It can also cause duplicative efforts in situations where resources are already limited.

Therefore child protective notification of law enforcement should be made as soon as there is reasonable cause to believe that the case falls within the statutory mandate or the provisions of an interagency protocol. Florida, for example, requires that

> if it was learned during the course of an investigation that [the observable injury or medically diagnosed internal] injury did occur as the result of abuse or neglect [the agency must] orally notify the state attorney and the appropriate law enforcement agency. In all cases, the department shall make full written report to the state attorney within three days of making the oral report.[59]

Ordinarily this determination is made when the initial report is received for investigation and the notification to the police made by phone to facilitate the initiation of a joint investigation. Deciding whether a notification is appropriate, however, is a continuing responsibility. Any time the child protective agency develops sufficient information to believe that the requirements for a notification are present, one should be made.

4

Investigations

The investigation of reports is but one part of a comprehensive community reponse to child maltreatment. Investigations must be conducted "as an integral component of a larger array of child welfare services designed to enhance the well-being of children, and of an even broader continuum of human services designed to meet the needs of children and families."[60] Because the investigation is often the first step in protecting children, however, it is important to establish clear investigative roles and responsibilities.

Concurrent and Joint Investigations

Investigation is a fact-finding process of interviewing, observing, and gathering evidence by which a report of suspected child abuse or neglect is verified and information gathered for decision making and possible court action. In cases of child abuse and neglect, the police bring expertise in collecting and preserving evidence, in examining the crime scene, and in taking statements and confessions.[61]

In the past many law enforcement agencies were hesitant to become involved in cases of child maltreatment.[62] Now law enforcement agencies are aware that their efforts are often required to protect a child from further maltreatment, and they are increasingly willing to investigate cases of child abuse and neglect. This change is to be applauded.

As described above, law enforcement is especially involved in "serious" cases where a prosecution seems likely. Most statutes concerning notification by a child protective agency to a law enforcement agency, for example, are attempts to specify a level of sufficient severity to justify police involvement.[63] Severity is not the only reason for police investigation, though. Other circumstances, usually dealing with the non-familial nature of the offense, may indicate the need for police involvement.

Because part of the police role is to assist child protective agencies, the scope of their investigations is not limited to matters that are admissible in a criminal prosecution. The police should seek as many facts as possible relating to the background and the circumstances of the setting in which the child has been endangered or abused. This information assists the police and the child protection agency in deciding whether further police action is indicated, whether the case should be referred for a prosecution, or whether it should be referred to a child protective agency or to some other agency better able to handle the particular problems involved, or, in the case of unsubstantiated reports, whether no further action is indicated.

The investigation by two or more agencies of the same case, along with interviewing the same parents, children, and other witnesses, requires careful coordination to prevent wasteful and potentially harmful duplication of effort. The Airlie House consensus-building group discussed this point:

> Child abuse is a crime and, therefore, a legitimate concern—and responsibility—of police and other law enforcement agencies. A number of calls made to CPS agencies may involve matters that are the sole or joint responsibility of law enforcement to evaluate and investigate. Recognizing this, there is a need to eliminate unnecessary multiple interviews of children and other unnecessary duplications of effort, to promote proper and expeditious collection and preservation of physical and other evidence, and to carry out the statutory mandate in the majority of states for law enforcement and

CPS agencies to cross-report such cases. Joint efforts with law enforcement—police and prosecutors—should be made to develop a coordinated system for identifying and investigating appropriate calls.[64]

Throughout the investigation the overriding concern of both law enforcement and child protective agencies must be the protection of the child. During joint investigations, however, child protective agencies must be sensitive to the pacing and scope needed by law enforcement to reach a positive prosecutorial outcome. Roles and responsibilities should be established to improve the effectiveness of the team effort and to reduce duplication. In some cases, for example, it may be appropriate for the child protective agency to defer to law enforcement the conduct of the first interview with the alleged offender, including its time and place. If so, the general results of the interview should be shared with the child protective agency.

Sharing information can raise additional concerns because, depending on the state, there may be more liberal discovery rules in either the civil or the criminal proceedings. Therefore child protective and law enforcement agencies should reach an understanding about what information each will record and make available to the other.

To address these and other issues, every community should develop a CPS-law enforcement protocol to help ensure coordinated child protective efforts. The elements of the protocol are described in the last part of this section.

Assistance to Child Protective Agencies

Even when the child protective agency conducts the investigation, law enforcement assistance may be needed. Although most maltreating parents are willing to cooperate with child protective workers, some are not. The police, for example, may be needed to deal with parents who are unwilling to allow access to their children or who refuse to permit their

25

TABLE 2: SITUATIONS SUGGESTING
THE NEED FOR PROTECTIVE CUSTODY

*These situations suggest the need for protective custody pursuant to
a court order or, if there is not time to obtain one, on an emergency
basis. The decision to remove a child, however, has a second part:
Can the need to place a child in protective custody be obviated by
the parent's incarceration or by the provision of appropriate social
services by the child protective agency or other agencies?*
*In any of these situations the younger the child, the greater is
the presumable need for protective custody.*

The child was severely assaulted, that is, hit, poisoned, or burned so
severely, that serious injury resulted or could have resulted. (The
parent, for example, threw an infant against a wall, but somehow
the infant was not seriously injured.)

The child has been systematically tortured or inhumanely punished.
(The child, for instance, was locked in a closet for long periods;
forced to eat unpalatable substances; or forced to squat, stand, or
perform other unreasonable acts for a long time.)

The parent's reckless disregard for the child's safety caused serious injury
or could have done so. (The parent, for example, left a young child
in the care of an obviously irresponsible or dangerous individual.)

The physical condition of the home is so dangerous that it poses an
immediate threat of serious injury. (Exposed electrical wiring or other
materials, for instance, create an extreme danger of fire, or upper-
story windows are unbarred and easily accessible to young children.)

The child has been sexually abused or sexually exploited.

The parents have purposefully or systematically withheld essential food
or nourishment from the child. (The child, for example, is denied

---

children to be examined by a physician or to be placed in
protective custody. If it appears that a child is in immediate
danger (see table 2) and there is no time to obtain a court
order, the police in all states have the authority to enter a
home forcibly, to take emergency protective custody of a
child, and to arrest a suspected abuser.[65]

TABLE 2:
CONTINUED

food for extended periods as a form of punishment for real or imagined misbehavior.)

The parents refuse to obtain or to consent to medical or psychiatric care for the child that is needed immediately to prevent or treat a serious injury or disease. (The child's physical condition, for instance, shows signs of severe deterioration to which the parents seem unwilling or unable to respond.)

The parents appear to be suffering from mental illness, mental retardation, drug abuse, or alcohol abuse so severe that they cannot provide for the child's basic needs. (The parents, for example, are demonstrably out of touch with reality.)

The parents have abandoned the child. (The child, for instance, has been left in the custody of persons who have not agreed to care for the child for more than a few hours and who do not know how to reach the parents.)

There is reason to suspect that the parents may flee with the child. (The parents, for example, have a history of frequent moves or of hiding the child from outsiders.)

There is specific evidence that the parents' anger and discomfort about the report and the subsequent investigation will result in retaliation against the child. (Such information could be gained through a review of the parents' past behavior, the parents' statements and behaviors during the investigative interview, or reports from others who know the family.)

The parents have been arrested for any reason, and there is no one to care adequately for the child.

SOURCE: Douglas J. Besharov, *Recognizing Child Abuse* (New York: Free Press, 1990).

A few parents can be dangerous to the child protective worker and others. Therefore, when a parent becomes belligerent or physically threatening, police assistance may be needed to protect the worker or otherwise maintain order. Situations of actual danger are no longer rare, and when they arise, the presence of the police can prevent a tragedy.

Child protective agencies can, and often do, seek police assistance without specific legislative authorization. After all, child abuse and neglect are crimes in all states, and the police have a general responsibility in such cases. But again there is a developing body of statutory law on the subject. About four states specifically require the police to assist child protective agency workers when they take a child into protective custody.[66] In addition about sixteen states have specific provisions that require police assistance in other situations.[67] Pennsylvania's statute, for example, provides that

> the secretary [of the department] may request and shall receive from . . . [law enforcement personnel] such assistance and data as will enable the department and the child protective services to fulfill their responsibilities properly. . .when assistance is needed in conducting an investigation of alleged child abuse.[68]

Although most police agencies seem willing to provide the needed assistance, as with after-hours emergency investigations, formalizing the ability of the child protective agency to call on law enforcement for assistance would help ensure that the help is available when needed. Therefore state law or the local CPS-law enforcement protocol should provide a procedure for the child protective agency to obtain law enforcement assistance. It should also specify the nature of the assistance and the relative decision-making responsibilities of both agencies.

Protective Custody

Some abused and neglected children face immediate danger of serious, and perhaps irreparable, injury if they are left at home (see table 2). For these children, removal from their home is in their best interests. (In this discussion protective custody includes placement with relatives.)

Although the police may have a general power to place endangered children in protective custody,[69] nearly all states give police officers a specific grant of authority to take children into protective custody without prior court approval.[70] About twenty states also give this power to child protective agencies.[71] As a practical matter, however, most do not attempt a forcible removal of the child without police assistance. This is good practice because the parent is less likely to react violently if police are present. About four statutes provide for police assistance in these circumstances.[72]

Authorizations to place a child in protective custody are generally limited to situations in which a child is in immediate danger or otherwise in need of immediate protection, care, or medical treatment and there is no time to apply for a court order.[73] A common construction is that the police may remove a child upon reasonable or probable cause to believe that the child will suffer immediate or imminent harm if not taken into custody.[74]

Ordinarily the decision to place a child in protective custody should be a joint decision with each agency valuing the judgment of the other. Child protective and law enforcement agencies, however, sometimes disagree about what to do. The key operational question is, Who decides?

The appropriate guide is state legislation. In those states in which the law gives child protective agencies the authority to remove children, the police should defer to the agency's judgment, and the CPS-law enforcement protocol should so provide. Conversely, in those states in which only police have authority to remove children, the ultimate decision must be made by the police, although significant weight should be given to the child protective agency's recommendation (either for or against removal). The agency's workers may know more about the family or may be able to offer services that obviate the need to remove the child. (The protocol should specify the nature and timing of this consultative process.)

In any event law enforcement should notify the child protective agency (and the court of competent jurisdiction) when a child is taken into protective custody, as statutorily required in about twelve jurisdictions.[75] Similarly, if there is a pending criminal investigation or prosecution and the child protection agency is contemplating the return of a child, before doing so it should consult with law enforcement for information and advice.

Sometimes a child is left at home because the suspected perpetrator has been jailed, but too often the perpetrator is subsequently released without notification of the child protection agency. This precludes a new assessment of the need to remove a child and can pose a great danger to the child. Therefore state law should provide that any court order incarcerating a defendant in a child abuse case contain an endorsement that the defendant is not to be released without notice to the child protective agency. Because of bureaucratic breakdowns, such notices are not always given, but partial compliance provides better protection than the present practice of no notice.

In some cases the danger to the child is so great that the need for protective custody is beyond question. But in less severe situations, decision making is much more difficult; there are no hard-and-fast rules. Table 2 lists the most common situations that suggest the need for protective custody.

Arrests

"Probable cause" is the ordinary standard for arrests by the police. For that purpose, it is defined as the reasonable belief that a crime has been committed and that the suspected person committed it.[76] But since almost all forms of child abuse, no matter how minor, are crimes, this is only the first step in deciding whether to arrest a parent.

According to the President's Commission on Law Enforcement and Administration of Justice, there is "an entirely proper conviction by policemen that the invocation of criminal sanctions is too drastic a response to many offenses."[77] As a result, police officers exercise discretion at almost every point in the criminal process, from deciding whether and how to investigate a complaint to determining the appropriate dis-

TABLE 3
CONDITIONS SUGGESTING THE NEED FOR AN ARREST

Subject to the provisions of state law and the existence of probable cause to believe that a crime was committed and that it was committed by the suspect, the following situations suggest the need to arrest the parent or other suspected perpetrator of the maltreatment:

When an arrest is needed to initiate a criminal prosecution

When a criminal prosecution seems likely (especially if there is reason to believe that the suspect will flee)

When the arrest of the suspect is the only way to reasonably ensure the child's safety

When the arrest of the suspect will sufficiently protect the child so the child need not be removed from the home

When an arrest may assist in the interview of the suspect

When the suspect's arrest is necessary to preserve the peace

NOTE: For the purposes of this list, arrest includes any time that an individual is placed in police custody regardless of criminal prosecution. Furthermore in some circumstances arrests are made when there was no initial intention to do so. A parent, for example, may be arrested for resisting efforts to gain entrance to the home to assess the child's situation.
SOURCE: Douglas J. Besharov, *Recognizing Child Abuse* (New York: Free Press, 1990).

position of a case and acquiring relevant evidence to support a prosecution.[78] Arrests for child abuse are no exception.

An arrest, besides setting the stage for a criminal prosecution, is also an important child protective device, as Jack Collins points out:

> The arrest of child-beating suspects accomplishes an important result—namely, an immediate change in the environment. Although this change is often temporary, it removes the offending adult from the environment, allowing the police to protect the child

31

from continued abuse and affords other agencies in the community an opportunity to initiate a more permanent rehabilitation program.[79]

An arrest with no follow-up—that is, when the parent is simply released—may further endanger the child, however, and may be detrimental to treatment efforts. Therefore an arrest must be approached with utmost care. If protective or restraining orders to keep the alleged abuser out of the home are enforceable, their suitability as alternatives should be carefully considered.

The major reason for an arrest is the appropriateness of a criminal prosecution, although a prosecution can be commenced without the suspect being taken into physical custody. For this reason the Attorney General's Task Force recommended that law enforcement agencies "presume that arrest, consistent with state law, is the appropriate response to situations involving *serious injury* to the victim, use or threatened use of a weapon, violation of a protection order, or *other imminent danger* to the victim" (emphasis added).[80] The other major conditions that suggest the need to arrest a parent are listed in table 3. Finally, although the arrest decision is basically within the province of law enforcement, the police (or prosecutor) should try to consult with the child protective agency before making the arrest.

5

Building Cooperation

Investigations raise major and recurrent questions about how best to coordinate law enforcement and child protective agency efforts. Coordination must be worked on constantly. Agencies will not always be successful, but even partial coordination can make a substantial improvement in the level of protection provided to endangered children.[81] As Wilson and Pence comment:

> Confronting the problem of the maltreatment of children requires the cooperation and coordination of professionals from a host of disciplines. Although we depend upon one another for information and action, few relationships are as potentially conflictual as that between the child protective service worker and the law enforcement officer assigned to investigate the same case. . . .
>
> The conflicts inherent in the relationship between CPS workers and police are serious but do not have to prevent our working together effectively. Communicating openly and formalizing the relationship where possible can break down the barriers to building a team that works for everyone: for the police, for CPS, and most importantly, for the child.[82]

Wilson and Pence make four recommendations:

1. Establish formal teams. Much conflict is overcome simply through familiarity and trust (although when personalities conflict the opposite may be true). Long-term teams can be established on community levels through mutual agreement of the team members or through state statutory changes.

2. Establish investigative protocols. Investigative protocols clearly lay out the roles and responsibilities of both police and CPS workers. This can be done even where no standing team agreement exists. Protocols limit conflict by clarifying expectations.

3. Provide adequate personnel to both agencies. The sources of conflict are amplified when a disparity exists in the personnel resources available to the two agencies. . . . Disparity in resources may also affect the individual level of commitment to the team concept, resulting in conflict.

4. Joint training. Joint training is a key once a team is established. It gives all parties an opportunity to hear the same message and learn skills together, and provides an opportunity to acquaint disciplines with each other's philosophical perspectives and unique difficulties. For example, discussion of the emphasis in law and policy on family preservation and visitation, as well as of the real limitations of the foster care system can enlighten law enforcement, while CPS can be sensitized to such issues as physical evidence collection, the subtleties of interviewing, and related areas. The training allows participants to reveal and resolve potential conflict.[83]

Multidisciplinary Teams

Child protective decision making, whether by child protective or law enforcement agencies, often entails a complex weighing of medical, social work, child development, and legal considerations. Decision making becomes easier, and more accurate, when it is made in consultation with other professionals whose skills and experience can help assess the situation.

For this reason the Attorney General's Task Force recommended that "communities should develop a multi-disciplinary team to investigate, process and treat all incidents of family violence, especially cases of physical and sexual abuse of children." The task force explained:

> To develop an effective coordinated response, each community should establish a multi-disciplinary team representing all agencies involved in family violence. Working together, team members can formulate a systematic approach with defined protocols that minimize the trauma suffered by the victim and maximize the opportunity to change the abusive patterns of the offender. . . .
>
> Communities must identify existing resources and bring together all groups addressing the problem of family violence at the local and state levels. A multi-disciplinary team made up of representatives of all agencies dealing with family violence can focus public attention on the seriousness of the problem and deliver the services necessary to meet the needs of the victims. This coordinated intervention by each jurisdiction can facilitate the most effective response to family violence incidents, particularly the sexual abuse of children and the elderly.[84]

Such cooperative efforts are the cornerstone to building more effective individual, as well as joint, protection of endangered children.

CPS-Law Enforcement Protocols

The statutory authority granted to law enforcement agencies, their operational capabilities, and the skills and expertise of individual officers make them an important element in the process of investigating child abuse and neglect.[85] How child protective and law enforcement agencies share this investi-

TABLE 4
ELEMENTS OF CPS-LAW ENFORCEMENT PROTOCOLS

Statement of purpose

Articulation of joint and respective missions and organizational responsibilities

Types of cases covered (for example, sexual abuse and serious or potentially serious cases of physical abuse)

Procedures for handling cases, including special investigative techniques

Criteria for child's removal

Criteria for arrest of suspects

Criteria for law enforcement referral to the child protective agency

Criteria for child protective referral to the law enforcement agency

Procedures to assist the child protective agency

Criteria and procedures for joint investigations, including timing, prime decision-making authority, and concurrent prosecutions

Provision for joint training

Provision for multidisciplinary team consultation

Criteria and procedures for cooperation and coordination among agencies

Provision for regularly evaluating the effectiveness of the protocol and modifying it as needed

gative responsibility depends on the type of situation and the community.

Therefore state law should require that every community have a CPS-law enforcement protocol jointly developed by the local child protective, law enforcement, and prosecutorial agencies. To the fullest extent possible, this should be a communitywide process with input from the full range of other human service disciplines and agencies. Even in the absence of such legislation, communities should adopt such protocols. (Table 4 lists the key elements of a protocol between child protective and law enforcement agencies.) Finally, since conditions may change, there should be a process for regularly evaluating the effectiveness of the protocol and modifying it as needed.

6
Conclusion

This report seeks to provide policy guidelines for improved cooperation and collaboration between law enforcement and child protective agencies in the handling of child abuse cases. Its most important findings and recommendations can be summarized as follows:

- Child abuse and child neglect are community problems requiring a cooperative response by law enforcement, child protective, and other local agencies. These agencies share the same basic goal: the protection of endangered children.
- Child protective agencies have become the primary recipients of reports of *intrafamilial* child abuse and neglect; all states have amended their reporting laws to require or allow reports to be made to them. The vast majority of reports are made to, and are investigated by, child protective agencies.
- Child protective agencies should encourage better reporting of suspected child abuse and neglect through public and professional education campaigns.
- Law enforcement agencies play an equally important role in a communitywide program for the protection of children through finding and reporting cases, assisting child protective agencies, investigating cases, placing children in protective custody, arresting perpetrators, and prosecuting offenders.
- Some cases require an immediate law enforcement response, and for this purpose the public should be able to make reports directly to law enforcement agencies.
- There should be careful efforts to improve coordination between child protective and law enforcement agencies so

that there is less chance of children falling between the cracks as each agency thinks the other is investigating a particular case.

• Regardless of any action taken by the law enforcement agency, state law or procedure should require it to report suspected intrafamilial child abuse and neglect to the child protective agency. (For, even if a criminal prosecution has been initiated, the immediate and long-term needs of all children in the family must be assessed and, if necessary, suitable substitute arrangements made.)

• In states that have adopted specific penal laws defining child abuse and neglect for criminal prosecutorial purposes, all cases falling under the statutory definition should be reported to law enforcement. In those states that have not adopted such laws, the severity of danger to the child (rather than of the severity of the actual injury) should guide decision making.

• Cases of nonfamilial child abuse and neglect should not be in the province of child protective agencies.

• State law should mandate that child protective and law enforcement agencies *at the local level* develop written agreements, or protocols, concerning the other types of situations that warrant an automatic notification to law enforcement.

• State law should also give local prosecutors the authority to obtain copies of any individual report or designated type or types of reports as they are received or at any time thereafter. (Such requests should be in writing.)

• State law or the local CPS-law enforcement protocol should guarantee that on a case-by-case basis child protective agencies are free to refer any other case they deem appropriate to either police or prosecutors, and they should be encouraged to do so.

• It is important to establish clear investigative roles and responsibilities between law enforcement and child protective agencies to improve the effectiveness of the team effort and to reduce duplication.

• Throughout the investigation the overriding concern of both law enforcement and child protective agencies must be the protection of the child.

- During joint investigations child protective agencies must be sensitive to the pacing and scope needed by law enforcement to reach a positive prosecutorial outcome. (In some cases, for example, it may be appropriate for the child protective agency to defer to law enforcement the conduct of the first interview with the alleged offender, including its time and place. If so, the general results of the interview should be shared with the child protective agency.)

- The decision to place a child in protective custody should be a joint decision with each agency valuing the judgment of the other.

- When there is a disagreement about the need to place a child, state legislation is the appropriate guide: in those states in which the law gives child protective agencies the authority to remove children, the police should defer to the agency's judgment. Conversely, in those states in which only police have authority to remove children, the ultimate decision must be made by the police, although significant weight should be given to the child protective agency's recommendation (either for or against removal).

- Arrests are an important child protective device. As the Attorney General's Task Force recommended, law enforcement agencies should "presume that arrest, consistent with state law, is the appropriate response to situations involving *serious injury* to the victim, use or threatened use of a weapon, violation of a protection order, or *other imminent danger* to the victim" (emphasis added).

- Coordination between law enforcement and child protective agencies on these and other matters must be worked on constantly.

- State law, therefore, should require that every community have a CPS-law enforcement protocol jointly developed by the local child protective, law enforcement, and prosecutorial agencies. To the fullest extent possible, this should be a communitywide process with input from the full range of other human service disciplines and agencies.

Notes

1. See generally D. Besharov, ed., *Protecting Children from Abuse and Neglect: Policy and Practice* (Springfield, Ill.: Charles C Thomas, 1988).

2. U.S. Children's Bureau, *Juvenile Court Statistics* (Washington, D.C.: U.S. Department of Health, Education and Welfare, 1966), p. 13.

3. S. Nagi, *Child Maltreatment in the United States: A Challenge to Social Institutions* (1977), p. 35.

4. American Association for Protecting Children, *1986 Highlights of Official Child Neglect and Abuse Reporting* (Denver: American Humane Association, 1988).

5. Compare U.S. National Center on Child Abuse and Neglect, *Study Findings: Study of National Incidence and Prevalence of Child Abuse and Neglect: 1988* (Washington, D.C.: U.S. Department of Health and Human Services, 1988), p. 3–11, table 3–5, estimating 1,100, with National Committee for Prevention of Child Abuse, *Child Abuse and Neglect Fatalities: A Review of the Problem and Strategies for Reform* (c. 1988).

6. J. Alfaro, "What Can We Learn from Child Abuse Fatalities? A Synthesis of Nine Studies," in Besharov, *Protecting Children from Abuse and Neglect*, pp. 219–64.

7. New York State Senate, Standing Committee on Child Care, *1985 Study of Child Protective Services* (Albany: n.d., c. 1986), p. 2.

8. See, for example, D. Besharov, "The Children of Crack," *Public Welfare*, vol. 47, no. 4 (Fall 1989), pp. 6–11.

9. U.S. Children's Bureau, *The Abused Child—Principles and Suggested Language for Legislation on Reporting of the Physically Abused Child* (Washington, D.C.: U.S. Department of Health, Education and Welfare, 1963).

10. The American Public Welfare Association estimates that about 15 percent of children whose abuse or neglect is substantiated are placed in foster care. Personal communication with Dr. Toshio Tatara, director, Research and Demonstration Department, APWA, February 13, 1989. See also U.S. National Center on Child Abuse and Neglect,

National Analysis of Official Child Abuse and Neglect Reporting (1978) (Washington, D.C.: U.S. Department of Health, Education and Welfare, 1979), p. 36, table 28, estimating that 20 percent of substantiated cases result in foster care or shelter care.

11. See D. Besharov, "Representing Abused and Neglected Children: When Protecting the Child Means Seeking the Dismissal of Court Proceedings," *Journal of Family Law*, vol. 20, 1981–1982, pp. 217, 218–19, 227–31.

12. The child's placement into foster care with the parent's consent is considered a voluntary service. Ibid., p. 228.

13. According to estimates of the American Humane Association, about 25 percent of all substantiated cases result in court action. American Association for Protecting Children, *1988 Highlights of Official Child Neglect and Abuse Reporting*, p. 42.

14. See M. P. Rosenthal, "Physical Abuse of Children by Parents: The Criminalization Decision," *American Journal of Criminal Law*, vol. 141, no. 7, 1979.

15. Attorney General's Task Force on Family Violence, *Final Report* (Washington, D.C.: U.S. Department of Justice, 1984), p. 10.

16. Ibid., p. 15.

17. Jack G. Collins, "The Role of the Law Enforcement Agency," in R. Helfer and C. H. Kempe, eds., *The Battered Child* (Chicago: University of Chicago Press, 1968), pp. 179, 186.

18. For example, Md. Fam. Law Code Ann. s.5-704(a)(1) (Supp. 1989); Or. Rev. Stat. s.418.755 (1989); D.C. Code Ann. ss.2-1352(c), 2-1353(a) (1988).

19. See, for example, National Center on Child Abuse and Neglect, *Study Findings: 1988*, pp. 6–12, table 6–4, showing that in 1986, 409,400 cases of potential abuse or neglect were reported to CPS. In that same year the police knew of only 96,700 such cases.

20. For example, Cal. Penal Code s.11166(a) (West Supp. 1990); Fla. Stat. Ann. s.415.504(2)(a) (West Supp. 1990); N.Y. Soc. Serv. Law s.415 (McKinney Supp. 1990).

21. S. Martin and D. Besharov, *Police and Child Abuse: New Policies for Expanded Responsibilities* (Washington, D.C.: American Enterprise Institute, 1990); S. Martin and E. Hamilton, *Policies, Procedures, and Issues in Law Enforcement Handling of Child Abuse Cases* (Washington, D.C.: Police Foundation, 1988).

22. A. Sedlak, *Supplementary Analysis of Data on the National Incidence of Child Abuse and Neglect* (Bethesda, Md.: Westat, 1989), p. 2–15, table 2–4.

23. See, for example, Ga. Code Ann. s.19-7-5(c) (1982 & Supp. 1989), Kan. Stat. Ann. s.38-1522(c) (1986) (when a child protective agency is unavailable); Alaska Stat. s.47.17.020(C) (Supp. 1989) (when

"the reporter cannot reasonably contact" the nearest child protective agency office, or when "immediate action is necessary for the well-being of the child"); Iowa Code Ann. s.232.70(2) (West 1985) (when "immediate protection for the child is advisable"); La. Rev. Stat. Ann. s.14:403 (D) (1) (West Supp. 1990) (when it is "necessary" to contact a law enforcement agency in addition to a child protective agency).

24. Iowa Code Ann. s.232.70 (2) (West 1985).

25. D.C. Code Ann. s.6-2103(d) (1989).

26. For example, Cal. Penal Code s.11166(g) (West 1982); Mich. Comp. Laws Ann. s.722.623(1) (West Supp. 1989); N.Y. Soc. Serv. Law ss.413, 415 (McKinney, Supp. 1990).

27. See note 18.

28. For example, Conn. Gen. Stat. s.17-38a(c) (Supp. 1989); Tenn. Code Ann. s.37-01-45 (1984); Wis. Stat. Ann. s.48.981(3) (West 1989).

29. Martin and Besharov, *Politics and Child Abuse*; Martin and Hamilton, *Policies, Procedures, and Issues*.

30. Ibid.

31. National Center on Child Abuse and Neglect, *Study Findings: 1988*, p. 6–12, tables 6–4.

32. Ibid.

33. National Center on Child Abuse and Neglect, *National Study of Incidence and Severity of Child Abuse and Neglect* (Washington, D.C.: U.S. Department of Health and Human Services, 1981), p. 34, table 6–2.

34. National Center on Child Abuse and Neglect, *Study Findings: 1988*, p. 6–12, table 6–4.

35. See for example, C. L. Willis and R. H. Wells, "The Police and Child Abuse: An Analysis of Police Decisions to Report Illegal Behavior," *Criminology*, vol. 26, 1988, pp. 695–715.

36. See generally D. Besharov and H. Asamoah, "The Statutory Framework for Police Activities in Cases of Child Abuse" (Washington, D.C.: American Enterprise Institute, 1988).

37. For example, Minn. Stat. Ann. ss.626.556(3)(a), (b) (West Supp. 1990); Neb. Rev. Stat. s.28-711 (1989); Tex. Fam. Code Ann. s.34.01 (Vernon Supp. 1990).

38. For example, Alaska Stat. s.47.17.025 (1984); La. Rev. Stat. Ann. s.14:403(d) (Supp. 1989); N.C. Gen. Stat. s.7a-548(a) (1989).

39. For example, Wash. Rev. Code s.26.44.030(3) (Supp. 1989) (physical injury).

40. For example, Del. Code Ann. tit. 16, s.905(a) (1983); Hawaii Rev. Stat. s.350-2(b) (Supp. 1989); Va. Code s.63.1-248.6(D)(5) (Supp. 1989).

41. For example, Fla. Stat. Ann. s.415.505(h) (1986 & West

Supp. 1990); Mass. Gen. Laws Ann. ch. 119, s.51B(4) (Supp. 1989); N.H. Rev. Stat. Ann. s.169-C:38 (Supp. 1988).

42. For example, Fla. Stat. Ann. s.415.505(h)(2) (1986).

43. For example, Mass. Gen. Laws Ann. ch. 119, s.51B(4)(c) (West Supp. 1989); N.H. Rev. Stat. Ann. s.169-C:38(I) (c) (Supp. 1988).

44. For example, Fla. Stat. Ann. s.415.505 (1986 & West Supp. 1990); Ind. Code Ann. s.31-6-11-11(d) (West Supp. 1987); Me. Rev. Stat. Ann. tit. 22, s.4013 (Supp. 1989).

45. For example, Me. Rev. Stat. Ann. tit. 22, s.4013 (Supp. 1989); R.I. Gen. Laws s.40-11-3.1 (Supp. 1989).

46. For example, Ala. Code s.26-14-7(d) (1986); Fla. Stat. Ann. s.415.505(1)(a) (1986); N.Y. Soc. Serv. Law s.424(4) (McKinney Supp. 1990).

47. For example, Ill. Ann. Stat. ch. 23, s.2054.1 (Smith-Hurd 1988); Wis. Stat. Ann. s.48.981(5) (West 1987).

48. Mass. Gen. Stat. Laws Ann. ch. 119, s.51B(4)(a), (b), (c), (d), (e) (West Supp. 1989).

49. Letter to Douglas J. Besharov, dated May 22, 1989.

50. More than three-fourths of the states have a specific cruelty-to-children statute. In the remaining states the traditional crime of assault, either statutory or common law, applies to child abuse. See generally M. Paulsen, "The Legal Framework for Child Protection," *Columbia Law Review*, vol. 66, 1966, pp. 679, 681.

51. For example, Kan. Stat. Ann. s.21-3609 (1986); Minn. Stat. Ann. s.260.315 (West 1986); Mich. Comp. Laws Ann. s.750.145 (Supp. 1989).

52. For example, National Center on Child Abuse and Neglect, *Child Protection: Guidelines for Policy and Program* (Washington, D.C.: U.S. Department of Health and Human Services, Office of Human Development Services, 1982), p. 84.

53. In 1987, a group of thirty-eight national experts on child protection met at Airlie House, Virginia, to develop guidelines for the reporting and investigation of child abuse cases. See "Child Abuse and Neglect Reporting and Investigation: Policy Guidelines for Decision Making," in D. Besharov, ed., *Protecting Children from Abuse and Neglect: Policy and Practice* (Springfield, Ill.: Charles C Thomas, 1988), chap. 13, p. 340.

54. For example, abuse in institutions and out-of-home care: Cal. Penal Code ss.11166(g), 11165.6 (West Supp. 1990); Fla. Stat. Ann. s.415.505 (1986 & West Supp. 1990); Minn. Stat. Ann. s.626.556(10a) (Supp. 1990). Minnesota, for example, requires police notification if the abuse is committed by "a person responsible for the child's care outside the family unit," which might include a parent's

live-in paramour, as well as day-care workers and teachers. (Minn. Stat. Ann. s.626.556 [10], [10a] [Supp. 1990])

55. Attorney General's Task Force on Family Violence, *Final Report*, p. 17 (emphasis added).

56. Letter to Douglas J. Besharov, dated May 22, 1989.

57. See the text at note 46.

58. For example, N.H. Rev. Stat. Ann. s.169-C:38 (Supp. 1987) (seriously injured); Tex. Fam. Code Ann. s.34.02(c) (Vernon 1986) (death).

59. Fla. Stat. Ann. s.415.505(g)(1) (1986).

60. "Child Abuse and Neglect Reporting and Investigation: Policy Guidelines for Decision Making," p. 2.

61. See generally R. Ruddle, ed., *Missouri Child Abuse Investigator's Manual* (Columbia: Juvenile Specialist Program of the Institute of Public Safety Education, University of Missouri, 1981), p. 79.

62. Besharov, *Protecting Children from Abuse and Neglect*, p. 494.

63. See notes 38–45.

64. "Child Abuse and Neglect Reporting and Investigation: Policy Guidelines for Decision Making," p. 3.

65. See the discussion in the next section and note 69.

66. For example, D.C. Code Ann. s.6-2105(a) (1989); Md. Fam. Law Code Ann. s.5-706 (1989); Utah Code Ann. s.62A-4-509(8) (1989).

67. For example, Kan. Stat. Ann. s.38-1523(b) (1986); Mich. Comp. Laws Ann. s.722.623(7) (Supp. 1989); Neb. Rev. Stat. s.28-713 (1989).

68. Pa. Stat. Ann. tit.11, s.2218 (Supp. 1989). Iowa imposes the requirement only in cases of abuse (Iowa Code Ann. s.232.71 [5] [West Supp. 1989]). In about twelve states the requirement extends to both cases of abuse and neglect. See, for example, Mich. Comp. Laws Ann. 722.623(7) (Supp. 1989); R.I. Gen. Laws s.40-11-9 (Supp. 1989); W. Va. Code s.49-6-10 (1986). In a few states assistance is required in special cases. Missouri requires police assistance in cases of sexual exploitation (Mo. Rev. Stat. s.210.145[5] [Vernon Supp. 1990]). The purpose of Vermont's requirement is "to assist in locating parents who have deserted their children and other persons liable for support of dependents" (Vt. Stat. Ann. tit.33, s.2553[a] [1981]).

69. This includes the authority to make a forced entry under exigent circumstances. See generally *Warden v. Hayden* 387 U.S. 294 (1967).

70. For example, Ariz. Rev. Stat. Ann. s.8-223(B) (Supp. 1989); Cal. Welf. & Inst. Code s.305(c) (West Supp. 1990); Wyo. Stat. s.14-6-205(a) (1986).

71. For example, Mont. Code Ann. ss.41-3-301(1), (3), 41-3-

1111 (1986); N.Y. Soc. Serv. Law s.398 (McKinney 1983); Tex. Fam. Code Ann. s.17.03 (1986).

72. For example, D.C. Code Ann. s.6-2105(a) (1989); Md. Fam. Law Code Ann. s.5-706 (Supp. 1989).

73. For example, N.Y. Family Court Act s.1024 (1983).

74. For example, Ind. Code Ann. s.31-6-4-4(c) (West Supp. 1987); N.Y. Family Court Act s.1024(a) (1983).

75. For example, Fla. Stat. Ann. s.415.506 (West 1989); Hawaii Rev. Stat. s.571-31 (Supp. 1989); Vt. Stat. Ann. tit. 33, s.641 (1981).

76. See, for example, W. LaFave and J. Israel, *Criminal Procedure* (1985), p. 110.

77. Kenneth C. Davis, *Discretionary Justice 83*, reprint 1980, pp. 86–7.

78. *Standards Relating to the Urban Police Function* (Chicago: American Bar Association, 1971), p. 120.

79. Collins, "The Role of the Law Enforcement Agency," p. 183.

80. Attorney General's Task Force on Family Violence, *Final Report*, p. 17 (emphasis added).

81. See, for example, B. Smith, "Coordinated Systems Response to Abuse of Children in Out-of-Home Settings" (Washington, D.C.: American Bar Association, 1988).

82. Charles Wilson and Donna Pence, "Professional Exchange: Facilitating Communication among Professionals," *Advisor*, vol. 1, nos. 1–4 (American Professional Society on the Abuse of Children, August 1988), pp. 2, 6.

83. Ibid., p. 4.

84. Attorney General's Task Force on Family Violence, *Final Report*, pp. 14, 15, 16.

85. C. J. Flammang, "Toward an Understanding of the Police Role in Child Protection," in Mary Urzi, ed., *Cooperative Approaches to Child Protection: A Community Guide* (St. Paul: Minnesota State Department of Public Welfare, 1979), p. 69.

Other Titles of Interest

Child Abuse: A Police Guide (American Bar Association, Police
Foundation, 1987)

Child Abuse and Neglect Reporting and Investigation (American
Bar Association, American Enterprise Institute, 1988)

*Family Violence: Research and Public Policy Issues (American
Enterprise Institute, 1990)

*Legal Services for the Poor: Time for Reform (American Enterprise
Institute, 1990)

Recognizing Child Abuse: A Guide for the Concerned (Free Press,
1990)

---

*Copies of these titles, as well as *Combating Child Abuse*, are
available at bulk rate from:

University Press of America
4720 Boston Way
Lanham, Maryland 20706
1-301-459-3366

The AEI PRESS is the publisher for the American Enterprise Institute
for Public Policy Research, 1150 Seventeenth Street, N.W., Washington, D.C. 20036: *Christopher C. DeMuth*, publisher; *Edward Styles*,
director; *Dana Lane*, editor; *Ann Petty*, editor; *Cheryl Weissman*, editor;
Susan Moran, editorial assistant (rights and permissions). Books pub-
lished by the AEI PRESS are distributed by arrangement with the
University Press of America, 4720 Boston Way, Lanham, Md. 20706.